ALAIN PROST

Alan Henry

Kimberley's

First printed: March, 1986
Published by: Kimberley's,
4 Church Close, London, N20 0JU
Editor: William Kimberley

Cover photos: Jeff Bloxham

First published: 1986
©Copyright Kimberley's
Printed by: The Lavenham Press Ltd., England

Alain Prost: ISBN 0 946132 30 5

United States distribution: Motorbooks International
Publishers & Wholesalers Inc
Osceola, Wisconsin 54020
USA

Contents

INTRODUCTION

It is somehow appropriate that one of Alain Prost's great racing heroes was Jim Clark. The Frenchman's six year quest to become the sport's first French World Champion has been characterised by the same meticulously unobtrusive style as the great Scottish ace of the sixties. Alain Prost showed style from the start of his Grand Prix career. Arriving in the Marlboro McLaren team at the start of 1980 as John Watson's team-mate, the reigning European Formula 3 Champion quickly asserted himself and was frequently quicker than his more experienced colleague. It was hardly surprising that he was wooed energetically by the French national Renault equipe with a view to switching camps in 1981. The courtship was brief and to the point: after his maiden year in the Grand Prix firmament, Prost left McLaren for home.

For the next three seasons he was always a Championship contender, coming within an ace of the title for his ambitions to be thwarted late in the year. But he won a total of nine races for the Regie before missing out on the '83 title by a mere two points to the Brabham-mounted Nelson Piquet. A destructive post mortem on the season's failure saw Renault and Prost split up a few days after the final race of the season, but while the French team locked into a steady decline which eventually led to its withdrawal from racing at the end of 1985, Alain's career shot skywards.

Rejoining the Marlboro McLaren International squad, Prost capitalised on John Barnard's brilliant TAG turbo-engined machine to win another twelve Grands Prix in 1984 and '85. In his first season back on the McLaren books, he lost out in the title chase to team-mate Niki Lauda, but sustained his winning ways into 1985 and finally became World Champion after finishing fourth in the Grand Prix of Europe at Brands Hatch.

A cosmopolitan European, not just a single-minded Frenchman, Prost and his family now make their home in Switzerland. For all his success, the diminutive Frenchman has kept his feet firmly on the ground and combines a sharp, endearing sense of humour with a keen perception of his worth as a Grand Prix racing driver.

EARLY DAYS

His early career including his first year in Formula One

Motor racing statistics may reflect stark, uncompromising race results, but they can be notoriously misleading barometers of true ability. Take Chris Amon, for example. One of the few men mentioned in the same breath as Jim Clark and Jackie Stewart during the late sixties and early seventies, the genial New Zealander eventually retired from the sport at the age of 33 without having scored a single Grand Prix triumph. Most people reckoned he ought to have notched up a dozen or more...

Of course, such justice is not always well served by a sport as technically complex as Grand Prix motor racing, but in the case of Alain Prost, victory in the 1985 World Championship merely topped off a stupendous five year run of success which started when he signed up with the French national Renault Elf team at the beginning of 1981. Race win followed race win to the point that he had nine Grand Prix triumphs in the bag by the time he quit Renault at the end of the 1983 season. Yet, having lost his Championship chance in the closing stages of each of those three years with the Regie, the even-tempered Alain began to accept that he might never take the elusive crown.

Yet his reward finally came at the end of the 1985 season; a canny fourth place finish in the Grand Prix of Europe at Brands Hatch was sufficient to throw the crown beyond the reach of his sole rival, Ferrari's Michele Alboreto. Yet, somehow, the realisation of that long hoped-for success was somehow swamped by the euphoria surrounding Nigel Mansell's first Grand Prix victory. After all those impressively dominant Grand Prix demonstration runs, Prost's greatest day had finally arrived at the end of a race during which the McLaren-TAG combination was less than fully competitive in *absolute* terms. Just as at the previous Grand Prix, the re-run Belgian race at Spa, Prost was cast in a supporting rôle. "It irritated me to have to drive like that," he admits, "because I always want to give of my absolute maximum. And as far as Spa was concerned, I started from pole and would have won easily if the track had been dry. But, with the Championship issue so close, I had to just sit on my enthusiasm and play things safe." This philosophy certainly paid off, but Alain would obviously have preferred to clinch his first World title win with a blisteringly dominant showing at the front of the field. The sort of performance of which he has, many times, proved himself capable.

1

3

2

Born on February 28, 1955 in the provincial French town of St. Chamond, just south of Lyons, Alain Prost's career progressed steadily onwards and upwards almost from the word go. Without doubt the little Frenchman with the crooked nose, this diminutive Charles Aznavour lookalike whose serious countenance was to earn him the soubriquet "Professor" during his time with Renault, has always displayed the Midas touch. In 1972 he began karting, by his own admission spending about a hundred dollars on his first machine. The following season he was picked up by a 'works' team and he steamed off to win the 1973 World Karting title. By

1976 he had clinched the hotly contested European Formule Renault Championship. He was one of the many recipients of financial and career support from the Elf petroleum concern, and eventually launched a serious assault on the European Formula 3 series at the wheel of a Martini MK27-Renault at the start of 1979.

Alain opened the contest by taking second place to Piercarlo Ghinzani's March 793-Alfa in the first race of the series at Rome's Vallelunga circuit, but as the Italian was ineligible to score points in the European series, Alain finished the day with a lead in the Championship table he was never to relinquish.

In the Preis von Knittelfeld, decided on an aggregate of two 12 lap heats round the Osterreichring, Prost turned the tables on Ghinzani to beat the Italian on the road, as well as in reality. Fifth in that race, at the wheel of a March 793-Toyota, was the man with whom Prost would dispute the 1985

World Championship contest - Michele Alboreto!

Prost beat Alboreto into second place at Zolder, scored another win at Magny-Cours and then ventured to Donington for the English round of the European series. Despite uncomfortably wet conditions, and unfamiliarity with the circuit, Alain's Martini came home third behind British F3 championship regulars Brett Riley and Chico Serra.

Alain's F3 season continued with victories at Monaco (commandingly), Zandvoort, Knutsdorp and Jarama, giving the Frenchman victory in the European Championship by 67 points with Holland's Michael Bleekemolen second (28 points), Sweden's Slim Borgudd third (23 points) and Italy's Mauro Baldi fourth (22 points). It was clear that the young Frenchman had considerable class and Prost decided to make the trip to the two North American Grands Prix at the end of the season in order to get his feet under the F1 table and make some crucially important new contacts.

The McLaren team was undergoing a pretty troubled phase at the time. At the end of 1978 Ronnie Peterson had been intending to join them as team leader, but his tragic death following that horrifying accident at the start of the Italian Grand Prix, had deprived the Marlboro-backed team of a crucial asset. John Watson was signed to take his place, but the Ulsterman suffered a frustrating 1979 season attempting to get to grips with the cumbersome M28, then worked hard to make progress with its mid-season successor, the M29. Watson's team-mate, Patrick Tambay, was to be dropped from the line-up at the end of the season, so McLaren boss Teddy Mayer was on the lookout for a replacement driver. It was against this back-cloth of uncertainty that Prost was introduced to Mayer by Marlboro's Paddy McNally in the pit lane at Watkins Glen. Marlboro France was at that time attempting to advance the careers of the country's Formula 3 graduates and McNally, who was based in Marlboro's Lausanne headquarters, was "holding Prost's hand" on this fact-finding trip.

"I thought 'who on earth was this little midget,'" smiles Mayer as he recalls that initial meeting. "I mean, the guy was no taller than me. I thought, 'he doesn't look anymore a racing driver than I do.' McNally asked us why we didn't give him a chance, so I arranged that he should have a go in the M29 at a Paul Ricard session shortly before the end of the year.

"On his first lap he was just warming up the car; on his second, he came through the right-hander before the pits in a full, opposite-lock slide; on the third, he equalled Watson's quickest lap in the same car... I didn't hang around to see anything else. I just ran for my car, grabbed a contract out of my briefcase and did the deal there and then..."

For all the tribulations which were to punctuate Prost's first season with McLaren, Mayer remained absolutely adamant "that it was obvious the guy

A pre-season test so impressed McLaren team boss Teddy Mayer that he there and then signed Alain up.

9

was that good, that soon..." Prost, quiet and self-effacing, seemed little more than a shy schoolboy when he appeared in the pits prior to the start of practice for the 1980 Argentine Grand Prix at Buenos Aires. Truth be told, the somewhat insular F1 world knew precious little about him. But he very quickly wiped the patronising grins off the faces of many rivals, quickly eclipsing team leader John Watson.

Prost's first two races saw him not only outqualify Watson on the grid, but score World Championship points quite comfortably. In the heat of Buenos Aires, Alain rounded off his FI debut with a sixth place finish, following this a fortnight later with fifth place in the Brazilian Grand Prix at Interlagos, defeating Arrows team leader Riccardo Patrese in a straight fight. That set the tenor of the season, although Alain suffered a temporary set-back when he fractured the scaphoid in his right wrist (a tiny bone, deep within the hand) after his M29B apparently suffered a rear suspension breakage and crashed heavily at the Esses. By dint of missing the United States GP West at Long Beach (where Stephen South deputised for him), the Frenchman gave himself

just eight weeks in which to recover before making a return to the cockpit for the Belgian Grand Prix at Zolder.

In terms of Championship points scored, Prost would only accumulate two more before the end of the season; one for sixth with the M29B at Brands Hatch, another for a similar placing first time out with the new, and less competitive, M30 at Zandvoort. In the meantime, he ran rings round Watson, particularly at Monaco where the Ulsterman failed to qualify, hard though it was to believe at the time. It was therefore no surprise that Prost's ability began to be envied elsewhere. Before the end of the season Alain had received an approach from Renault and, despite vociferous and understandable objections from McLaren - which was just in the process of amalgamating with Ron Dennis's Project Four organisation to form McLaren International - the Frenchman went off to drive for his home team.

Prost always seems cautious when this particular matter is raised, although he does concede to having felt "uncomfortable" during his first stint with the McLaren team. To add to his Kyalami shunt, he also went off during practice at Watkins Glen, his M30 charging

1. Alain's first Grand Prix was the Argentinian in which he outqualified team-mate John Watson. 2. Alain only scored 5 championship points in that first year, but had made a big impression on other teams. 3. From the start, he was a clever and thoughtful driver.

1

straight on at a fourth gear left-hander. On race morning he was still suffering from giddy spells, but took part in the untimed warm-up session before prudently withdrawing from the race following a somewhat strained exchange with the team management.

Mayer recalled: "I think by the end of the year he was rather disillusioned with us. I reckon that one of those accidents was down to us possibly, the other down to him. But by the end of the year it was clear that Renault was pursuing him pretty hard and the whole thing was getting slightly unpleasant. We considered suing Renault over this business, because we had a continuing deal with Alain, but the matter was eventually settled out of court when Renault paid us off. I was sad that things ended like that, but that does not in any way alter the regard I developed for Alain as a driver. He was a very clever racing driver, first and foremost. He figured out the business of being competitive and successful very quickly indeed and, most importantly, he was not only very fast, but easy on the car as well. What followed came as no surprise to me: he was that good..."

3

2

RENAULT

Three years with the French national team

Just as René Arnoux eclipsed Jean-Pierre Jabouille at Renault, so Alain Prost eclipsed René Arnoux. That's the way it looked in 1981, for certain. Prost came in to replace Jabouille, the veteran Frenchman having sustained very serious leg injuries in an accident during the 1980 Canadian Grand Prix at Montreal. Arnoux had two wins to his credit in 1980, but Prost was clearly set to make him work even harder the following year.

The first two Prost/Renault outings were catastrophic. A collision with Andrea de Cesaris's McLaren wrote Alain out of the US GP West at Long Beach on the very first corner, while he was punted off the road in the rain-soaked Rio race by Didier Pironi's spinning Ferrari. The third race was the Argentine GP at Buenos Aires, Alain qualifying second to Piquet's controversial Brabham BT49C and eventually finishing third behind Nelson and Carlos Reutemann's Williams FW07C. Arnoux trailed home a dejected fifth.

The advent of the superb new Renault RE30, which made its race debut in the Belgian GP at Zolder, underlined the fact that Prost's first race victory could not be long coming. The portent was correct: although team-mate René Arnoux slammed round Dijon-Prenois to start the French GP from pole posi-

1

2

tion, it was Alain Prost who took the chequered flag. But this was a race result not without its controversy.

With 22 laps remaining, a torrential downpour had sent cars skating in all directions and resulted in the race being stopped at a point where Nelson Piquet's Brabham was leading from John Watson's McLaren and Prost's Renault. Goodyear had only returned to the Grand Prix fray that weekend following a temporary "political" withdrawal prompted by the destructive FISA/FOCA war the previous winter which had been sparked by FISA's decision to ban sliding skirts in an attempt to reduce cornering speeds. The Akron tyre company had nothing in the way of soft compound qualifying rubber available for its competitors, so the Michelin runners were rubbing their hands with glee at the prospect of a "second heat" over the remaining 22 laps to the finish.

Prost, however, was worried. "I had been having difficulty selecting fourth gear and I really didn't know whether it would stand up to that last sprint to the flag. I already held third place and was worried that I might be about to lose that if the race continued. But the race continued and, for some reason I'll never understand, that fourth gear worked perfectly all the way to the finish."

3

1. When Alain joined the Renault team in 1981, he eclipsed his experienced team-mate René Arnoux. 2. However his first two outings were catastrophic. Driving the RE20B, he had accidents in both Rio and Long Beach. 3. The advent of the superb new Renault RE30 underlined the fact that his first Grand Prix victory could not be long coming. 4. Alain with Gerard Larrousse (centre) and René Arnoux.

4

1. Alain debuted the RE30 in the Belgian GP at Zolder. 2. At Zandvoort, now with his first Grand Prix win under his belt, he battled hard for much of the race with Alan Jones's much more agile Williams FW07C to win his second Grand Prix.

His first Grand Prix triumph now tucked tightly under his belt, Prost continued to be a front-running contender for the remainder of the year, but Renault unreliability snatched victories from his grasp at Silverstone, Hockenheim and Osterreichring. At Zandvoort he battled hard for much of the race with Alan Jones's much more agile Cosworth-engined Williams FW07C to win his second Grand Prix and then

won again at Monza, putting it over Jones yet again. With two races left to run, Prost was 12 points adrift of Championship leader Carlos Reutemann. It was a long shot, but just possible. As it turned out, a retirement at Montreal followed by a second place finish at Las Vegas behind Jones's Williams, was not sufficient for Alain to become France's first World Champion. He failed by just seven points.

1

2

Of course, at this stage in his career, there was a marked reluctance on the part of many observers to give Prost due credit for his driving ability. We were going through a phase when it was fashionable to dismiss anybody with turbo power as a "point and squirt merchant". It would take another couple of seasons before Alain's truly outstanding talent would become universally appreciated.

4

3. He won again at Monza.
4. Even now, Alain's outstanding talent was still doubted by some.

3

With two races left to run in 1981, Alain still had a chance of winning the Championship. However, he failed by just seven points.

1

1. Alain started from the front row of the grid in the thinly supported San Marino Grand Prix of 1982 having already won the season's two opening races. (Photo J. Townsend). 2. However an engine failure wrote him out the race. 3. The following race at Zolder, he slid off with worn tyres.

The Renault driver line-up for 1982 remained unchanged and great things were expected from the RE30Bs when they were unloaded at Kyalami to contest the opening race of the season. Off-track, the debate centred round the notorious "super licence" dispute which threatened the race to the point where the drivers locked themselves away in a Johannesburg hotel and refused to return to the circuit until some sort of compromise was worked out with the sport's governing body. Eventually all was well and Arnoux qualified on pole ahead of Nelson Piquet in the debutant Brabham-BMW BT50, Gilles Villeneuve's Ferrari 126C2, Riccardo Patrese's Brabham-BMW and Prost. During practice the BT50s had been the stars of the show, topping 200mph on the long rush down to Crowthorne corner, but when the starting light blinked green, both Ecclestone's machines made poor starts and it was Arnoux and Prost who led through the first corner pursued by the two Ferraris.

Prost took over the lead from his team-mate on lap 14, but Alain's apparently untroubled victory run turned sour when he headed for the pits to change a deflated rear tyre at the end of lap 41 resuming the chase in eighth place. On his fresh Michelins he proved more than a match for his rivals, clawing back to regain the lead nine laps from the finish to win from Carlos Reutemann's Williams FW07C and Arnoux, the second Renault slowing towards the end thanks to badly worn tyres.

Surely there was no way Prost could be stopped in his quest for the World Championship in 1982? Despite a misfiring engine, Prost came in third behind Piquet and Rosberg in the Brazilian GP at Rio, inheriting victory after the two English cars had been disqualified at the start of what turned out to be the seemingly eternal brake cooling "water bottle" controversy. In order to keep in terms with the more powerful turbos, English FOCA-aligned teams (still predominantly reliant on the normally aspirated Cosworth DFV) tried to drive a loophole through the technical regulations. Renault protested their efforts and the first two cars home at Rio were removed from the results. Prost and France's national racing team would need more assistance than that to win a World Championship, however.

Locking brakes sent Alain into the wall at Long Beach and an engine failure at Imola wrote him out of the thinly supported San Marino GP (which was boycotted by the FOCA teams) which was won by Pironi's Ferrari against team orders. Then Renault began throwing away the World Championship as if for effect: Alain slid off with worn tyres at Zolder and then crashed hard at Monaco's notorious chicane almost within spitting distance of the chequered flag. Not another single race victory awaited Alain for the balance of the 1982 season, although team-mate Arnoux would bag two, the French and the Italian.

2

3

1. Alain started from the front row 9 times in 1982, including 5 pole positions. 2. At Brands Hatch, Alain won another point with sixth place. 3. However, 1982 for Alain was disappointing scoring only two wins.

3

The problems of attempting to run a Formula 1 team as an extension of Renault's corporate PR department, while at the same time keeping two highly competitive drivers content, was highlighted by their 1-2 result at Paul Ricard. Put simply, René had won against team orders, although there were many who agreed with the way in which he had handled himself during this crucial event on home soil.

Alain still retained an outside chance of snatching the Championship, but that opportunity was fast disappearing by

1,2. At Zandvoort, the Renaults started from the front row as usual, but it was Didier Pironi, in the Ferrari (No. 28) who won the race after both were in trouble soon after the start. Photo 2 by John Townsend). 3. Despite their four wins in 1982, the season was a failure for Renault as both drivers often failed to finish in the other races. 4. Alain had to settle for fourth in the Championship.

1

2

3

the time the two Renaults lined up together on the front row at Paul Ricard. René had outqualified Alain on this occasion, but he agreed that he would do everything to aid Alain's Championship aspirations, even to the point of conceding the lead if they found themselves running 1-2 in the closing stages of the race.

After fleeting challenges from Brabham and Ferrari faded away, that is precisely what happened. But Alain, grappling with understeer caused by a broken side skirt, had dropped to more than twenty seconds adrift with ten laps to go. Arnoux just could not bring himself to sit on his racer's instincts and kept ahead to the flag. Said René, "If Alain had been right on my tail, it would have been different. But I just couldn't bring myself to slow down that much..."

Prost faced his obvious disappointment with quite a remarkable degree of stoicism, taking the company line and mouthing all the right sentiments - "what is important is that Renault has won" - at the post-race briefing. Privately he was furious. "I could have run quicker, despite that broken skirt, but there was no need to do so because I was trusting him to slow down," explained Alain, "I thought I could trust his word..."

4

1

1. The first two years with Renault left Alain with a reputation difficult to assess.
2. His meticulous style flattered the machinery at his disposal. 3. It was the result of the French GP, which Arnoux won against team orders, that destroyed the relationship between Alain and his teammate. (Photo by Rougier Press).

2

3

1

To say that relations between Prost and Arnoux were never quite the same again would be something of an understatement. Discreetly, Alain let it be known that he was not terribly interested in having Arnoux on team strength as his partner in 1983. René was not worried: by the time he won at Paul Ricard his new deal with Ferrari was being finalised behind the scenes. The two men would not drive together again.

Renault had introduced its own fuel injection system as from the Monaco GP, where their staggering performance on this tight circuit could be attributed largely to this crucial new development which centred around an electronically controlled Kugelfischer-Bosch mechanical pump. But from that point onwards, this aspect of the technical specification became Renault's great bugbear, letting down the cars time and time again. Amazingly, Alain continued to remain reasonably philosophical about the whole affair.

2

Those first two years at Renault left Prost with a reputation as a difficult driver to assess. His meticulous style had flattered the machinery at his disposal, projecting the impression that he was a tidy driver, yet perhaps lacking the passionate fighting spirit which is the hallmark of a truly great driver. In other words, if Prost won, then it was down to the superb performance of his car: if he lost, as at Monaco or Paul Ricard, it was because he made an error and crashed or Arnoux was simply quicker. Subsequent events were to show that assessment short-changed Alain to a quite unjust degree.

Of course, as history would eventually relate, Renault's moment had passed by the end of 1982. The marque had just completed two seasons in which they *should* have won the World Championship, but their cars consistently succumbed to mechanical failure. In 1983 the priority was to produce more power allied to much improved reliability. This was achieved, but too late. The Renaults were by now fighting against the tide of increasingly competitive challenges from rivals such as Ferrari and Brabham-BMW. The technical regulations had been changed to require flat-bottomed chassis and the new RE40 was not ready for the first race of the season - nor fully sorted when Alain gave it that debut at Long Beach.

In retrospect, this was another example of the Renault team's poor reaction time. In Brazil, Nelson Piquet had a brand new Brabham BT52 at his disposal - and won, first time out with it. Alain struggled home seventh with the outclassed RE30C at Rio and then finished out of the points again at Long Beach, the unsorted RE40 obviously an improvement over the older car, but not quite ready for front line action. When the history books were written it could be seen that Brabham's maiden victory with the BT52 was a crucially important step in winning Nelson Piquet his second World Championship. Renault's tardy start to the year, by the same

1. Alain Prost and Renault team boss Gerard Larrousse. (Photo by John Townsend). 2. Alain completely dominated the 1983 French GP in his RE40. (Photo by William Kimberley). 3. In Belgium, Alain stormed to yet another victory.

1

2

1. Alain's success in the 1983 French GP made up for his disappointment of the previous year. (Photo by Rougier Press). 2. At Monaco, Alain was troubled by a faulty fourth gear and had to give way to Rosberg and Piquet to finish third. 3. The 2 North American races did not bring much encouragement for Alain, scoring only 2 points altogether. It was not until he reached Silverstone that his fortunes changed again.

3

token, was a major contributory factor in preventing Prost from taking the title.

When the European season started, Prost at least made up for his initial disappointments by completely dominating the French Grand Prix at Paul Ricard. His RE40 was on pole position by almost two seconds, a testimony to his superb driving talent as much as the excellence of the chassis, and Alain quite simply dominated the race. Routine fuel/tyre stops were *de rigeur* in Formula 1 at the time and the Renault mechanics did him proud when it came to servicing his car, Prost only briefly relinquishing the lead to Nelson Piquet's Brabham when he made his stop. At Rio the Brabham-BMW had seemed to be the class of the field, so Prost's victory with the RE40 on this super-fast circuit seemed to herald a World Championship at least.

Eddie Cheever was Alain's teammate for 1983 and the Italian-resident American backed up Prost well with a strong run to third place at Paul Ricard and there were several other occasions on which he showed promisingly in the top six. At Montreal, with Prost troubled by an electrical gremlin, Eddie rose superbly to the occasion and stormed home second behind René Arnoux's Ferrari. It is supremely ironic that Cheever's career suffered, albeit obliquely, as a result of being partnered with Alain. The sceptics who believed Alain was over-rated therefore came to the conclusion that Cheever, inevitably slower than the Frenchman, was nothing more than a moderately competent journeyman. Too late, for Eddie Cheever at least, came Alain's move to McLaren International. The 1984 season would prove that Prost was, in fact, under-rated, a fact which also shed retrospective light on Cheever's performances. But by then he had been dropped from the Renault squad and faced two years languishing, uncompetitively, at Alfa Romeo.

1. Throughout the summer of '83, things got steadily better for Alain. 2. Alain won the British Grand Prix in champion style. (Photo by Gordon Dawkins). 3. In Holland, having just won the Austrian GP, Alain stumbled. As he braked while passing Piquet, he locked up his wheels and slid into the Brabham. Although he did not go off himself, half a lap later his car understeered into the guardrail. (Photo by Rougier Press.)

Throughout the summer of '83, things got steadily better for Alain Prost. His immaculate style was ideally suited to the revamped Spa-Francorchamps circuit and he stormed to a convincing victory in the Belgian Grand Prix after a freak front-running performance by Andrea de Cesaris in the fast, yet fragile, Alfa 183T ended with alleged gearbox failure. The two mid-summer North American races netted him only a spin and eighth place at Detroit followed by a troubled fifth at Montreal, but he won in champion style again at Silverstone, demonstrating impeccable form on the super-fast Northamptonshire circuit.

Arnoux's Ferrari romped away to win at Hockenheim, but Prost underlined that he wasn't averse to wheel-banging aggression at the Osterreichring, where he battled successfully against both Piquet and Arnoux to win. Standing on the victory rostrum that afternoon, Alain looked as though he was on the verge of a World Championship - and if anybody had predicted that this was the last race the works Renault team would win before its withdrawal from Formula 1 more than two years later, that prophet of doom would have been dismissed as an uninformed crank.

The Renault public relations machine was now beginning to get into top gear. Huge advertising billboards carrying the "Allez Alain" messages were plastered across many French cities as he nurtured his 14 point lead in the World Championship table. There were plans afoot for a whole planeload of French journalists to be flown to Kyalami, the last race of the season, to watch him win his Championship for France and for Renault should the contest last that long. The whole system seemed geared to accept that the Championship battle would go all the way, but there was never any doubt in Renault's mind that, at last, this time they were going to put it in the bag!

1

2

3

1

Privately, however, Alain felt slightly worried after the Austrian Grand Prix. "We had some detailed discussions with the management at about this time and I warned everybody that BMW was making tremendous strides in terms of horsepower." Alain recalls, "I realised that we needed to make a big effort unless we were going to be eclipsed in the last few races of the season. Looking back, I'm not certain that they took my warnings seriously enough..."

Not that Prost was blameless - no driver ever can be. The next round of the title chase, Zandvoort's Dutch Grand Prix, saw Alain make a vital stumble. Piquet's Brabham BT52B rushed off into the lead at the start of the race, but Alain gradually hauled him back just as the time was approaching for the spate of routine refuelling stops.

"I was anxious to get in front of Nelson because I didn't want to have to follow him into the pit lane," Prost explained, "I figured that time lost in the pit lane might be crucial and whoever was first out, on new tyres, stood the best chance of winning the race. People

think I took a chance, but I didn't think that was the case. It seemed a perfectly logical decision to take..."

The lap prior to his scheduled pit stop, Prost attempted to outbrake Piquet into the Tarzan right-hander. He came into the corner on a perfectly sensible line, taking a tight approach towards the apex; just as it appeared that the manoeuvre was complete, the Renault began to slide, tail-out to the left. Prost slightly over-corrected and, in an instant, had made contact with Nelson, nudging the Brabham into the protective tyre barrier on the outside of the corner. But Prost survived - almost certainly because he had been able to lean on his Championship arch-rival.

However, if Renault fans thought their man had got away with a lucky escape, they were quickly proved wrong. Mid-way round the same lap, Alain got off-line cresting a rise: the Renault's damaged front, right aerofoil, shredded in the impact with Piquet, did not give him the downforce he needed, and the RE40 slid oh-so-gently off into the guard-rail. He was out of the race.

1. By now, the Renault publicity machine was beginning to get into gear since Alain still had a 14 point lead with only 3 races to go. (Photo by Robert Young). 2. After Monza, where Alain retired and Piquet won, his lead was down to 5 points.
Overleaf: Although Renault achieved more power and more reliability in 1983, the engines became unreliable after rebuilds and contributed to Alain failing to win the Championship.

2

"I still think the Championship will be OK," smiled Alain rather thinly, trying to bolster his own self-confidence when the press corps descended on him after the race. But, inwardly, he was very worried about that Brabham-BMW, Nelson Piquet was fast emerging as the man of the moment: the Brazilian was "hot", and Prost fully appreciated what that might mean in the three remaining races.

Monza was next on the calendar and there was a fair deal of anti-Alain feeling brewing up in Italy when he arrived for the Italian GP. Whether it was just anti-Renault feeling in general, or simply the fact that Arnoux still held an outside chance of winning the title for Ferrari, is not clear. Anyway, Prost went to Monza protected by a couple of burley bodyguards. His RE40 retired and Piquet won the race. Alain's advantage was now down to five points.

The penultimate round of the Championship took place at Brands Hatch

under the title Grand Prix of Europe. Prost's RE40 was again outgunned by Piquet's Brabham BT52B, although this time the Frenchman hung on to finish second to the Brazilian. One race to go and Alain had only two points in hand. Nelson had to beat him pretty convincingly at Kyalami, so, in theory, Alain still held the advantage. But the whole trend was running against Renault by now and Prost knew it.

Optimists to the end, Renault still packaged up droves of French journalists and despatched them on expensive trips to Kyalami. It was a vain effort. Brabham pulled an ace card, gambling to start with an unusually light fuel load, pull out a mammoth lead in the opening stages, then stop for fuel early and hope to retain an advantage right through that pit stop. It worked brilliantly. By the end of lap three Piquet had destroyed the opposition precisely to plan. He could even afford to drop back to third at the chequered flag.

1. Even after winning his 4th Grand Prix of the season at Austria, Alain was still worried. Nelson Piquet was "hot" and was emerging as the man of the moment.
2. Alain knew he had his work cut out if he was to keep ahead of Piquet in the Championship.

1

2

Prost's breathless Renault failed to last the distance, crawling into retirement with turbo failure. Some cruel observers suggested that Alain deliberately retired rather than face a straight defeat at Piquet's hands. That was maliciously unfair. Prost was in no way bitter that Piquet had won the Championship, merely annoyed that Renault had been so dilatory in response to his warnings about the

BMW power increases. Nelson, from his vantage on the winner's rostrum, generously paid tribute to Prost's efforts over the year, the Brazilian making it plain that Renault, not Alain, had allowed the Championship to slip away.

Prost recalls, "In those days it got to a point where just about anything I said at Renault was wrong. Everybody was concerned about the corporate image and you had to be very careful about what was said in public if you were not to upset anybody. It became very difficult." The difficulty was not destined to last very long.

In a remarkably self-destructive post mortem on the season's racing programme, Prost found himself facing his critics back in Paris a few days after Kyalami. It did not take long to discover that there was no point in continuing their relationship.

Brands Hatch was the scene of the European GP. Piquet won and Alain came second to take six more valuable points.

McLAREN

His next two years culminating in becoming World Champion

Alain was out of work barely a day or so. His relationship with Renault Sport boss Gerard Larrousse had plummeted spectacularly during his final year driving for the Regie: in fact, whatever the outcome of the Championship struggle, there was already considerable doubt over whether Alain would remain with the team. With all the accumulated bitterness now brimming over, he quickly announced that he would no longer be driving for them.

There had been rumours that things were going bad on Prost. The Formula One "bush telegraph" is remarkably accurate and searching. Over at Marlboro, the McLaren team's major sponsor, senior executives were

After leaving Renault at the end of 1983, he was barely out of work a day or so, being quickly snapped up by McLaren International. (Photos by Rougier Press, left, and Auto-foto, bottom).

monitoring the position carefully. John Watson was haggling over his contract terms, so there was a vacancy, *technically*, at any rate. Once Prost indicated that he was free, Marlboro and McLaren moved with the speed of light. By Friday following the South African Grand Prix, Prost had been signed to drive alongside Niki Lauda for 1984. Watson was out of Formula One work!

Facing up to double World Champion Lauda was quite an experience for Prost, for although the Frenchman had no doubt about his own abilities, he confessed that there was something slightly daunting about opening a partnership with a man whose reputation as an individualist was so marked.

Prost smiles: "Of course, Grand Prix racing is always tremendously competitive, but I suddenly appreciated

that it would be a whole lot *more* competitive working in a team with Niki. When I arrived at McLaren International, to be honest I was not totally certain about what I would find. I knew that I was going to work, to fight, to my absolute maximum - and I knew that fight would include everybody, Niki as well.

"I understood that if I proved myself quick enough to justify my place in the team, then I need never have any worries about the equipment I would be given. The season held every bit as much promise as it did for him..."

Prost describes Lauda as "scrupulously honest." Lauda, at the time, was a little more wary, remarking, "we both have the same driving styles, so when we test together, or agree a chassis set-up, it can quickly be transferred from one car to the other. As far as his driving ability is concerned... if

November, 1983 and Alain joins his new team-mate Niki Lauda at a testing session at Paul Ricard. (Photo by John Townsend).

you have a team-mate as competitive as Prost certainly is, well, you've just got to find some means of beating him..."

The finalised 1984 McLaren-TAG MP4/2 was only readied shortly before the start of the new season, so when Prost went out and scored a first time out victory at Rio, it represented the best possible tonic for the hard working team operated by John Barnard and Ron Dennis. It also laid to rest any doubts about Prost's ability.

In the immediate post-Renault period, there was resentment and bitterness in France surrounding Prost's defection to McLaren. Even in his home town of St. Chamond he found his prized Mercedes 500SEC had been vandalised and there were defamatory accusations that he had cheated on his

income tax. It was not long before Alain took his wife Anne-Marie and their three year old son Nicholas to a new home in Switzerland. Even when he finally clinched his World Championship title at the end of 1985, Alain admits that he did not feel overtly *French* when he considered his attitude to winning the title. A cosmopolitan European, Alain won the Championship for himself, first and foremost...

The Rio victory was sweet, no question about it. "It was tremendously important that I should win rather than Renault because it finally buried all the aggravation between us. If they had won in Brazil, I would have been in trouble with the French press putting on the pressure, very quickly. As it was, the pressure started to be focussed on Renault..."

Alain's first race with his new team resulted in victory, in Brazil. (Photo by John Townsend).

1

1. Joining the McLaren team, Alain would prove to many of his critics just how under-rated he had been while with Renault.
2. For much of the season, the race wins swung backwards and forwards between Lauda and Alain.
3. His third Grand Prix victory of the year was at Monaco.

2

3

For much of the 1984 season the race wins swung backwards and forwards between Niki and Alain. Lauda won at Kyalami, then Dijon and Brands Hatch. Prost passed the flag first at Monaco. Then Niki won at Brands Hatch, where Prost retired with gearbox trouble. That was the breakthrough that the Austrian had been waiting for. It moved him to within a point and a half of Prost's total and set the stage for a rivetting second half to one of the most fascinating seasons in recent Formula 1 history.

Unquestionably, Prost was quicker than Lauda. Quickly adapting his technique to get the best out of the TAG turbo V6 - "It had a bit more throttle lag than the engines I'd been used to, but otherwise it was just fine" - Alain could match anything that Niki did in challenge. At Hockenheim and Zandvoort they played cat and mouse with each other, but on both occasions Alain came out on top. They went into the final round of the Championship, at Estoril, each with a sporting chance. But Niki was three and a half points ahead. If Alain won the race, Niki would have to be lower than second. He wasn't! Prost did everything that was expected of him, but Niki won the Championship by a scant half-point margin, the slimmest in the 35 year history of the title chase.

It had been Alain Prost's most successful season by far. He had won seven races to Lauda's five, driven through the entire field after a late start in the spare car from the Kyalami pit lane and also won at Hockenheim after a last-moment switch to the spare. Lauda won only five, yet clinched the Championship. Statistics seem meaningless under these circumstances.

In the Monaco GP, Alain was shadowed by Nigel Mansell's Lotus which darted into the lead on lap 11, but then crashed out of the race 6 laps later. By the end of the race, Alain was again in danger of being over-taken, this time by Ayrton Senna in the Toleman, but in the appalling conditions, the race was stopped prematurely.

1. Alain is seen squirting champagne at Jean-Marie Balestre, President of FISA, motor sport's governing body, in celebration of his victory at Hockenheim, his 4th of the season.
2. At the Nürburgring, Alain clocked up his 6th victory of the season.

1

3

1. Alain qualified on the front row of the grid for the British GP, but failed to finish while Lauda won. 2. In Germany, the McLarens of Alain and Lauda finished a magnificent first and second with fastest lap to Prost as a bonus. 3. Alain won his 5th Grand Prix of the season at Zandvoort, beating Lauda by just 10 seconds. 4. In the pre-race warm-up for the European GP at the Nürburgring, Alain got his left rear wheel over the edge of the track and promptly spun. He missed the wall of tyres but hit a Rescue Car instead. Despite all this, he actually won the race.

4

1

Prost was pleased when he heard that Lauda would be staying on for 1985, not moving over to Renault as had been rumoured around Monza time. "I can accept the fact that Niki has won the title and I have not," reflected Prost thoughtfully, "but I know I can win it next year. What really matters to me is the atmosphere of trust which has built up between us. We definitely worked as a team. When we faced Piquet as our only serious challenger in the British Grand Prix at Brands Hatch, we agreed that, if one of us should get by, he would wait for the other one to follow him through past the Brabham rather than making a break for it immediately. And

1. Alain won the Portuguese GP, the final race of the season in 1984, but Lauda, by coming second, won the Championship by a scant half point. He is seen on the winner's podium being hugged by McLaren boss, Ron Dennis. 2. Prost was pleased when he heard that Lauda would be staying on for 1985. (Photo by Autofoto). 3. Alain duplicated his previous year's victory at Rio, the first race of the season in 1985. (Photo by John Townsend).

2

3

Niki was never difficult about letting me use the spare car. He was completely honest and you knew exactly where you were with the man."

Alain was anxious to continue into the 1985 season in the same successful vein as he had departed from the previous one. "It's tremendously important to sustain your competitive edge year after year," he insists, "I don't want to get into the sort of position we've seen Nelson trying to handle: one year he's up and winning lots of races, the next year he's struggling. I would hope to be a contender for the Championship every year, even if I don't always make it."

For 1985 John Barnard took an essentially conservative route, updating the MP4/2 into 'B' specification, incorporating new rear suspension, revised aerodynamics and a stronger gearbox. Its build programme took place, once again, alarmingly close to the first race of the season, but Alain duplicated his previous year's victory to perfection. He started the season with a win so, although the TAG turbo was not the quickest from a sheer qualifying point of view, the combination of Porsche and Bosch technology continued to make it the most fuel efficient, and generally effective, unit over a full race distance.

For 1985, John Barnard, the McLaren designer, took a conservative route updating the MP4/2 into 'B' specification.

1. First lap and Senn[a] and de Angelis have already gone, follow[ed] by Alain, Michele Alboreto's Ferrari, Warwick's Renault, Lauda, de Cesaris, Tambay, Piquet and Johansson.
2. Ghinzani's lapped Osella separates Ala[in] from the pursuing Fe[r]rari of Alboreto.
3. Although the TAG turbo was not the quickest from a she[er] qualifying point of view, the combinatio[n] of Porsche and Bos[ch] technology continue[d] to make it the most fuel efficient, and generally effective, unit over a full race distance.

3

1,2. In Portugal Alain uncharacteristically fell foul of the diabolical conditions.

3. "One of the most difficult cars to drive on such a tight circuit" was Alain's reaction to the Monaco race having just won it.

4. Alain relaxes with his wife and close friends. 5. An engine pick-up problem dropped Alain to third place on the last lap behind Piquet and Rosberg in the French GP.

Ayrton Senna speedboated to victory in the Portuguese Grand Prix at Estoril, leaving Prost, uncharacteristically, to fall foul of the diabolical conditions and spin his McLaren into retirement on the main start/finish straight. At Imola, Prost spent most of the San Marino Grand Prix jousting wheel-to-wheel with Senna, but the Lotus ran out of fuel and the McLaren was first past the chequered flag. Sadly, the Frenchman was subsequently disqualified when his MP4/2B was found slightly underweight at post-race scrutineering.

Alain took the decision stoically, although he was clearly very disappointed as he had derived more

satisfaction from the Imola win than possibly any other race. "I was very pleased with the way I drove at Imola, although you can hardly describe it as a true race because fuel economy was such a crucially important issue. I battled with Senna for as long as I dared, but eventually I had to call it off when it looked as though I might be in consumption trouble. I calculated everything just perfectly and ran out of fuel on the slowing down lap..."

Monaco followed next with Alain starting from the third row of the grid, effectively finishing the job he had started 12 months earlier. In the rain-soaked half-points 1984 Monaco race,

1

2

3

4

5

he had struggled home a few lengths ahead of Senna's fast-closing Toleman. Now he battled with Michele Alboreto's Ferrari 156/85, beating the Italian car convincingly after Michele was obliged to stop to change a deflated rear tyre. What we did not know from the touchlines at the time was how difficult Alain's task actually was. A sticking turbocharger boost control valve on one cylinder bank of the TAG V6 made throttle response tricky in the extreme. "One of the most difficult cars to drive on such a tight circuit I have ever experienced," he remarked with evident self-satisfaction once the race was complete.

Third place behind the two Ferraris at Montreal was followed by an unexpected driving error at Detroit where, grappling with fading carbon fibre brakes, he slid into one of the retaining walls and out of the race. An engine pick-up problem, with which he grappled for much of the race, dropped Alain from second to third on the last lap of the French Grand Prix at Paul Ricard, but his level headedness with regard to fuel consumption paid off in the British Grand Prix at Silverstone where he refused to be drawn into a battle with Senna's Lotus and eased off when he realised things were getting marginal. Ayrton ran out of fuel, Prost won...

He spun at Nürburgring, but finished second to Alboreto's Ferrari and won again at the Osterreichring after Niki Lauda's sister car retired whilst leading when a turbo lost boost pressure. At Zandvoort, where the abrasive nature of the track surface meant that just about everybody had to stop for tyres, Alain had a longer pit stop than expected and plunged back into the race behind team-mate Lauda who had stopped early on. He hauled back onto the Austrian's tail, but Niki was pulling every trick in the book and kept him behind to the chequered flag.

Alain found his car beautiful to handle at Paul Ricard. (Overleaf).

1,2,3,4. On his final warm-up lap at the Austrian GP, Prost went off the road at the Hella-Licht chicane when the throttle stuck open. (Photos by Autofoto). 5. He went on to win the race.

1

2

3

4

5

"I think it's good for Niki's morale that he should have had a win like this," Alain grinned afterwards. Going into the Italian Grand Prix at Monza, Prost had 56 points to Alboreto's 53, so the contest was still wide open - in theory. The reality was rather different. Ferrari's chassis development programme had lost its way and the Italian driver was floundering. At the start of the year his 156 had virtually been a match for the McLaren in terms of untemperamental handling, but the Maranello engineers had gone off down the wrong track. They were in the wilderness.

Monza was ruled by the Willams-Hondas for most of the race distance, both Keke Rosberg and Nigel Mansell demonstrating blindingly quick form. But neither managed to survive to the end, leaving Prost to duck through and take the victory. Alboreto retired, so the

Frenchman was now eight points ahead. "I was contentedly sitting in second place thinking that I was doing well if I came home runner-up to the Honda," grinned Prost, "but then Keke retired and I was handed the win on a plate. Frankly, it was more than I expected, but I'm delighted about it nonetheless!"

Now it was simply a question of rolling home gently, taking no risks and buttoning up the title as quickly as possible. Alboreto retired again at Spa, but Prost finished third from pole position. He sat on the true racer's instincts again at Brands Hatch, fourth place being sufficient to confirm him as World Champion before making the long treks to South Africa and Australia for the final two races of the year.

Alain was delighted with the accolades he received from the even-

Prior to his pit stop, Alain led the Dutch GP from Niki Lauda. However, the positions were reversed after the stop for tyres.

handed British enthusiasts. "I was touched by how pleased they seemed to be for me, both at Silverstone and Brands Hatch. I seem to be more popular in England than I am in front of my own home crowd. Certainly more popular than I was when driving for Renault!"

Thus, at the end of the 1985 title chase, Alain Prost had become the first French World Champion, an achievement which perhaps lacked the nationalistic fervour that it might have attracted in the fifties or sixties, but a supremely worthy achievement by a highly competitive and thoroughly competent driver. Truly, in this case, the best man had won!

History will judge Prost to be one of the supremely talented drivers of his era, although I suspect he is even better than most of his peers give him credit. In a five year winning span, he notched up a total of 21 Grand Prix victories and is not finished yet, not by any means. His contract with McLaren International extends through until the end of 1987, by which time it would be reasonable to expect him to have topped Jackie Stewart's career record of 27 victories.

On a personal level, Alain likes his privacy with people he knows and trusts. His closest friend in the Formula 1 game is Jacques Laffite, the wiry, 41 year old Ligier driver who shares the ownership of a golf course near Dijon with the new World Champion. One of the writer's most vivid recollections of the 1985 season is watching Laffite help unload Prost's baggage outside Montreal's Meridien hotel just prior to the Canadian Grand Prix weekend. They were like a couple of schoolboys out on a weekend treat together!

Ron Dennis and John Barnard both realise the asset McLaren International has on its hands in Alain Prost. "An instinctive racer," Dennis describes him as. Barnard points out that "you really know where you are with Alain. He can be relied upon to give his all during testing at any particular circuit and his memory for chassis settings is quite remarkable by any standards. He is a constant factor in the equation based on which you can *always* tell where you are."

The 1986 season will see Alain Prost paired with Keke Rosberg now that Niki Lauda has decided to retire from the cockpit - this time almost certainly for good. Faced with the prospect of the Flying Finn competing from within his own team, Alain simply smiles and says "I think it will be good for the both of us." Somehow Keke's sheer flair stands out like a beacon, but the 1982 World Champion knows he will have to work hard to beat the 1985 title holder.

I suspect the '86 season will show Alain Prost in an even more favourably competitive light than ever before - and that those few doubters will be silenced once and for all.

At the end of 1985, Alain Prost had become the first French World Champion.

1

2

1. Nine more points for Prost - Monaco '85.
2. Another full score at Silverstone. 3. He had to be content with 'only' second place at the Nürburgring.

EVENT	RACE NUMBER	CAR	GRID POSITION	RACE RESULT
1980				
Argentinian	8	McLaren M29	12th	6th
Brazilian	8	McLaren M29	13th	5th
S. African	8	McLaren M29	22nd	DNS Crashed, injured wrist during accident.
Belgian	8	McLaren M29	19th	DNF Transmission
Monaco	8	McLaren M29	10th	DNF Accident at Ste. Devote.
Spanish	8	McLaren M29	6th	DNF Engine
French	8	McLaren M29	7th	DNF Transmission
British	8	McLaren M29	7th	6th
German	8	McLaren M29	14th	11th
Austrian	8	McLaren M29	12th	7th
Dutch	8	McLaren M30	18th	6th
Italian	8	McLaren M30	24th	7th
Canadian	8	McLaren M30	12th	DNF Accident/suspension failure
U.S.	8	McLaren M30	13th	DNS Withdrew after race morning warm up.

World Championship of Drivers: 15= (5 pts)

EVENT	RACE NUMBER	CAR	GRID POSITION	RACE RESULT
1981				
U.S. (West)	15	Renault RE20	14th	DNF Hit by de Cesaris
Brazilian	15	Renault RE20	5th	DNF Hit by Pironi
Argentinian	15	Renault RE20	2nd	3rd
San Marino	15	Renault RE20	4th	DNF Gearbox
Belgian	15	Renault RE30	12th	DNF Clutch
Monaco	15	Renault RE30	9th	DNF Engine
Spanish	15	Renault RE30	5th	DNF Accident
French	15	Renault RE30	3rd	**1st**
British	15	Renault RE30	2nd	DNF Engine
German	15	Renault RE30	1st	2nd
Austrian	15	Renault RE30	2nd	DNF Front suspension
Dutch	15	Renault RE30	1st	**1st**
Italian	15	Renault RE30	3rd	**1st**
Canadian	15	Renault RE30	4th	DNF Accident with Mansell
Caesars Palace	15	Renault RE30	5th	2nd

World Championship of Drivers: 5th (43 pts)

EVENT	RACE NUMBER	CAR	GRID POSITION	RACE RESULT
1982				
S. African	15	Renault RE30B	5th	**1st**
Brazilian	15	Renault RE30B	1st	**1st**
U.S. (Long Beach)	15	Renault RE30B	4th	DNF Accident; brakes
San Marino	15	Renault RE30B	2nd	DNF Engine
Belgian	15	Renault RE30B	1st	DNF Accident
Monaco	15	Renault RE30B	4th	7th
U.S. (Detroit)	15	Renault RE30B	1st	Running, not classified
Canadian	15	Renault RE30B	3rd	DNF Engine
Dutch	15	Renault RE30B	2nd	DNF Engine
British	15	Renault RE30B	8th	6th
French	15	Renault RE30B	2nd	2nd
German	15	Renault RE30B	2nd	DNF Fuel injection
Austrian	15	Renault RE30B	3rd	8th
Swiss	15	Renault RE30B	1st	2nd
Italian	15	Renault RE30B	5th	DNF Fuel injection
Caesars Palace	15	Renault RE30B	1st	4th

World Championship of Drivers: 4th (34 pts)

1983

Brazilian	15	Renault RE30C	2nd	7th
U.S. (Long Beach)	15	Renault RE40	8th	11th
French	15	Renault RE40	1st	**1st**
San Marino	15	Renault RE40	4th	2nd
Monaco	15	Renault RE40	2nd	3rd
Belgian	15	Renault RE40	1st	**1st**
U.S. (Detroit)	15	Renault RE40	13th	8th
Canadian	15	Renault RE40	2nd	5th
British	15	Renault RE40	3rd	**1st**
German	15	Renault RE40	5th	4th
Austrian	15	Renault RE40	5th	**1st**
Dutch	15	Renault RE40	4th	DNF Accident damage
Italian	15	Renault RE40	5th	DNF Turbo
European	15	Renault RE40	8th	2nd
S. African	15	Renault RE40	5th	DNF Turbo

World Championship of Drivers: 2nd (57 pts)

1984

Brazilian	7	McLaren MP4/2	4th	**1st**
S. African	7	McLaren MP4/2	5th*	2nd
Belgian	7	McLaren MP4/2	8th	DNF Distributor
San Marino	7	McLaren MP4/2	2nd	**1st**
French	7	McLaren MP4/2	5th	7th
Monaco	7	McLaren MP4/2	1st	**1st**
Canadian	7	McLaren MP4/2	2nd	3rd
U.S. (Detroit)	7	McLaren MP4/2	2nd	5th
U.S. (Dallas)	7	McLaren MP4/2	7th	DNF Hit wall
British	7	McLaren MP4/2	2nd	DNF Gearbox pinion bearing
German	7	McLaren MP4/2	1st	**1st**
Austrian	7	McLaren MP4/2	2nd	DNF Spun off
Dutch	7	McLaren MP4/2	1st	**1st**
Italian	7	McLaren MP4/2	2nd	DNF Engine
European	7	McLaren MP4/2	2nd	**1st**
Portuguese	7	McLaren MP4/2	2nd	**1st**

World Championship of Drivers: 2nd (71½ pts)

1985

Brazilian	2	McLaren MP4/2B	6th	**1st**
Portuguese	2	McLaren MP4/2B	2nd	DNF Spun off
San Marino	2	McLaren MP4/2B	6th	Disqualified
Monaco	2	McLaren MP4/2B	5th	**1st**
Canadian	2	McLaren MP4/2B	5th	3rd
U.S. (Detroit)	2	McLaren MP4/2B	4th	DNF Brakes/accident
French	2	McLaren MP4/2B	4th	3rd
British	2	McLaren MP4/2B	3rd	**1st**
German	2	McLaren MP4/2B	3rd	2nd
Austrian	2	McLaren MP4/2B	1st	**1st**
Dutch	2	McLaren MP4/2B	3rd	2nd
Italian	2	McLaren MP4/2B	5th	**1st**
Belgian	2	McLaren MP4/2B	1st	3rd
European	2	McLaren MP4/2B	6th	4th
S. African	2	McLaren MP4/2B	9th	3rd
Australian	2	McLaren MP4/2B	4th	DNF Engine

*Started from pit lane

World Championship of Drivers: 1st (73 pts - best 11 results)

Born: 24th February, 1955 at Saint Chamond (Loire).
1971:   Started karting as both a mechanic and driver.
1972:   Gave up his studies to devote himself to karting.
1973:   Official driver of SOVAM, probably one of the first professional karting drivers in France.
1974:   French and European karting champion.
1975:   Received a grant from the French Automobile Federation which helped him to attend the Winfield
           school at Paul Ricard which consequently enabled him to win the title of 'Elf driver' in November.
1976:   Winner of the Formula Renault Challenge (12 victories out of 13 races, 11 lap records).
1977:   Winner of the European Formula Renault Championship.
1978:   French Formula 3 champion.
1979:   European Formula 3 champion and winner of the Monaco Grand Prix Formula 3 race.